Contents

Listening walk

These children are on a listening walk.

- They can hear the hedge rustle.
- They can hear the birds sing.
- They can hear the traffic.
- They can hear an aeroplane.

Your teacher is going to take you on a listening walk.

✿ What will you hear on your listening walk?

✿ Draw what you heard.
Write about what you heard.

✿ Use Task Sheet 1.

What can you hear?

🔹 Listen to the tape.
Spot the sounds.

YOU NEED:

tape of different sounds

🔹 Use Task Sheet 2 to draw or write what the sounds are.

🔹 When do you hear these sounds?

🔹 How do you know what they are?

What sounds?

✿ Look at these musical instruments.

✿ How can you make sounds with them?

pluck	hit	shake
stroke	twang	blow
rattle	tap	scrape

✿ Complete Task Sheet 3.

What instrument is this?

✻ Here are some musical instruments.

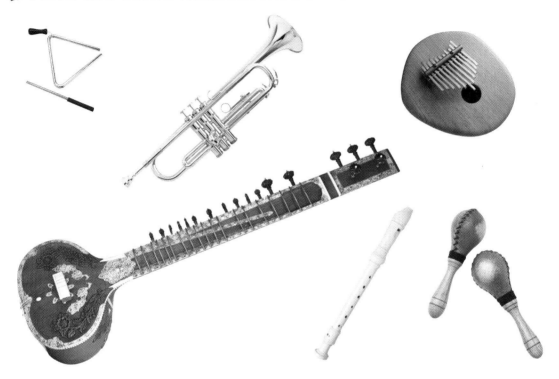

triangle	recorder	thumb piano
maracas	sitar	trumpet

✻ Try to match the name to the instrument on Task Sheet 4.

5

5 Describe your sound

Listen to a sound.
Then tell somebody what you heard.

Use words like these:

musical

high

loud

low

quiet

noisy

soft

6

Task 6 **What do you feel?**

✦ Put your hand on your throat gently.

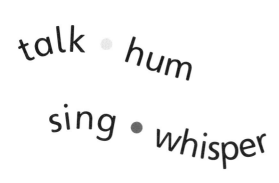

✦ What do you feel?

✦ Use words like these to describe what you feel:

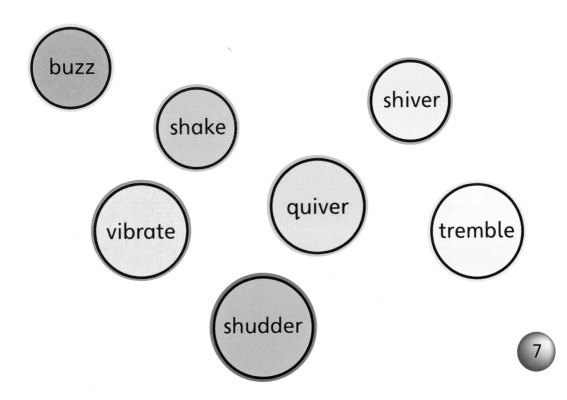

buzz

shake

shiver

vibrate

quiver

tremble

shudder

Scientific Enquiry

Stopping the sound

✪ Find ways to stop sound reaching your ears.

✪ Write what you find in the boxes on Task Sheet 5.
We call these boxes a **table**.
Put your results in a table.

How we stopped the sound	What we could hear
With one hand	
With both hands	
With ear muffs	

8 Who hears well?

Always cross the road carefully.

✿ Are all these children crossing safely?

✿ Which children are safe?

✿ Why are the others in danger?

✿ Complete Task Sheet 6.

Task 9 Investigating sound

These children are investigating sound.
They are walking away from the sound.
They are seeing how the sound changes.

 What are they measuring?

 What do you think they can hear?

Make a table

The children recorded their results in a table:

What the bell sounded like	How far away we were
The bell was very loud	1 cone
The bell was quiet	2 cones
The bell was very quiet	3 cones
We could not hear the bell	4 cones

What do you think the results show?

✿ Make your own sound investigation.

✿ What do you think will happen?

✿ Make your own table to record your results.
   This table has been started.
   Finish it on Task Sheet 7.

What we could hear	
loud	
	2 cones
very soft	4 cones

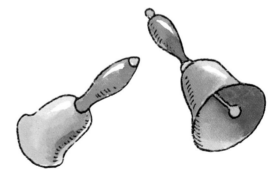

11 Make a block graph

8

✺ Make a block graph of your results on Task Sheet 8.

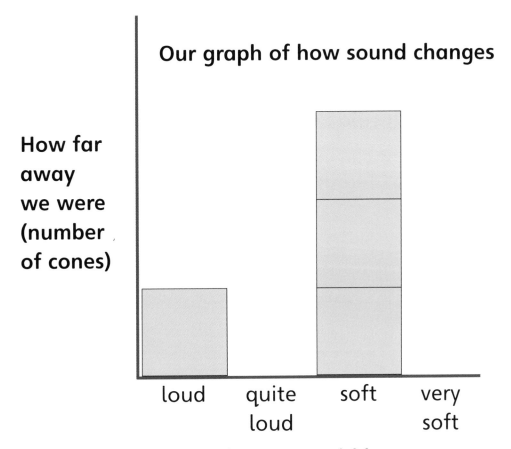

Our graph of how sound changes

How far
away
we were
(number
of cones)

loud   quite   soft   very
       loud   soft

What we could hear

✺ What did you find?

What shall we tell Ted?

Ted wants to play with his band.
But Mr Brown does not want to hear them.

✿ What should Ted do?

Ted wants to play in the park.
He wants all the people to hear him.

✿ What should Ted do?

✿ Send a message to Ted.
Tell him what to do.

⚡ Answer the questions on Task Sheet 9.

⚡ What have you found out?

⚡ What sort of things make sound?

⚡ What happens when you make a sound with your mouth?

⚡ How can you stop sounds reaching your ears?

⚡ When is it dangerous to stop sounds reaching your ears?

⚡ What happens to sounds as you get further away from them?

The School Band

Clash! Bash! Scrape.
Ting! Ting! Shake.
These are the sounds
Our instruments make.
Click. Click. Clack.
Bish! Bash! Boom!
These are the sounds
That fill the room.

✪ List the sounds in the
poem.

✪ What instrument could
make each sound?